Little Zaid's Journey to Salah

A Children's Book Introducing the Ritualized Islamic Prayer

by The Sincere Seeker **Kids** Collection

Salam Alaykum, friend! My name is Zaid, and I am 10 years old. Alhamdulillah, I am proud to say that I pray five times a day to Allah. But I'll let you in on a little secret. I did not always start praying 5 times a day. It was quite a journey to get where I am today. Along the way, I learned a lot, and I have to admit, I struggled a bit too—it was not as easy as I thought it would be. But it was worth it. I am a much better person now, and I feel great!

I have some news for you! I want to take you on a ride down memory lane to see the path and journey I took to get to where I am now. I promise you'll love it and learn a lot from it, just like I did. And you'll be excited and look forward to your prayers every day! Come on and join me! I'll see you on the next page where it takes us back to when I was seven years old!

'Son, come join me and have a seat,' said my dad. 'Now that you are old enough, it is time to learn about one of the most important things you'll ever learn and do,' added my dad.

'Wow, that sounds pretty serious, Dad, I am ready to hear!' I replied to my dad.

'Son, we are Muslims, we believe and worship Allah, our Creator, the Creator of you and I, the Creator of this whole world and everything in it. One of the most important ways of Worshipping Allah is praying to him every day, five times a day. Praying to God is the second pillar of Islam. Praying to Allah is called 'Salah' in Arabic, and it means 'connection.' Can you guess why, Zaid? asked my dad.

'Hmm… is it because, in Salah, we connect with Allah?'

'That is correct, son!' replied my dad, patting me on my head.

'Salah is our way to connect with Allah throughout the day, so we can build and have a good relationship with the One that created us, the One that loves us so much! When we pray, we ask Allah for guidance to show us the straight path to living a good life in this world and get us closer to Him so we can be with Him in the next world,' said my Dad.

'Zaid, I have a surprise for you tomorrow, we'll be going somewhere very special,' said my dad.

I immediately stood up. 'Where? Where are we going, Dad?' I asked with full excitement.

'You'll find out tomorrow, Zaid,' said my dad.

'Zaid, come down here, son, today is Friday, and we are going to that special place I told you about yesterday,' said my dad.

I ran down the stairs, 'Ready, ready!!' I shouted.

'Before we go, I have a surprise gift for you, Zaid.'

'Two surprises in one day??' I asked, barely holding my excitement.'

'That's right son, I told you today was going to be a special day for you. Go ahead and open your gift, son.'

I opened the gift, it was a beautiful white garment that goes down to the ankles.

'This is called a '*Thobe,*' son. Go try it on, and let's head out,' said my dad.

I tried it on and hopped into our blue family van and fastened my seat belt as we drove for about ten minutes or so, then my dad announced, 'We are here!'

I looked around and noticed a lot of people parking their cars and walking into this beautiful white building with a green dome on top. Many of them were wearing Thobes, just like my dad and me. As we walked into this beautiful white building--- we walked into the prayer area, which had stunning red carpet all around and lines formed one after the other. There were a lot of people, some praying, and some sitting down.

'This is called a Mosque, or Masjid in Arabic, son,' said my dad. 'This is one of many of Allah's houses. Muslims come here to pray every day to Allah, especially on Friday--- the blessed day of the week,' said my dad. 'Now before we pray, we need to make ablution-- called Wudu in Arabic,' added my dad.

'What's that?' I asked my dad in confusion.

'Wudu is what Muslims perform before they pray-- a Muslim is required to clean and purify themself by washing their hands, face, arms, head, and feet. It's important that a Muslim cleanse themselves, have clean clothing, and a clean area where they pray. Now, let's enter the wash area, you can watch me perform Wudu and copy what I do, son,' said my dad.

After we washed, we entered the prayer area. On Fridays, there is a sermon that the Imam – the person who leads us in prayer—gives before we pray.

'The sermon will start in 2 minutes, have a seat, son,' said my Dad.

As my dad and I sit, someone got up, adjusted the microphone, and announced the Adhan, the Islamic chant or call of prayer given before prayer to call people to come to pray. The Imam's sermon was about the importance of Salah and why we perform Salah.

'We worship Allah because he deserves to be worshipped because of who He is. He is the Only One that is in full control of everything. He is All-Powerful, All-Wise, All-Knowing, All-Hearing. We also worship him to thank him for creating us and providing us with everything we have.' Said our Imam.

After the sermon was over, we all prayed together as a group after the Imam. We prayed facing the direction of Mecca, where the Holy House of God is—known as the Kaaba.

Muslims from all over the globe face this direction, which was the first house that was built on Earth for the worship of the One God. Of course, we do not worship the Kaaba, we only use this Holy House as a direction to face while worshipping the One God. Prayers are only directed to God, our Creator.

After we finished praying, we headed home.

'Dad, that was beautiful, I loved it-- Allah's House is so beautiful and peaceful, I can't wait to come back again!' I said to my dad.

'You'll be seeing more of Allah's house, inshAllah!' said Dad as we drove home.

As we got home, I saw my big sister and mom praying together in the living room. When they finished, my big sister Zara told me that she wanted to teach me something. She said she wanted to go over the movements of the Salah.

'Salah is not merely praying or supplicating to God by just speaking our minds—rather, it requires certain sayings and movements that we learned from our last and final Prophet, Muhammad, peace be upon him. We were commanded to pray, just like Prophet Muhammad taught us.' Zara said.

She showed me how the prayer starts with 'Allahu Akbar,' which translates as 'God is Greater (than everything),' and she demonstrated how the prayer involves the recitation of Verses from the Holy Quran, as well as praises and supplications to God, all while standing, bowing and prostrating to Him.

'Make sure to make a lot of dua (supplications) to Allah when you are in prostration (sujood) because we are the closest to Allah when we are in that position,' said Zara.

'So, feel free to ask Allah for Paradise and whatever else you want in the hereafter and in this world!' she added. 'You should pray, Zaid, just like the hundreds of millions of people all around the globe do,' said my sister.

When we finished, I gave her a hug for teaching me how to pray and got myself ready for lunch.

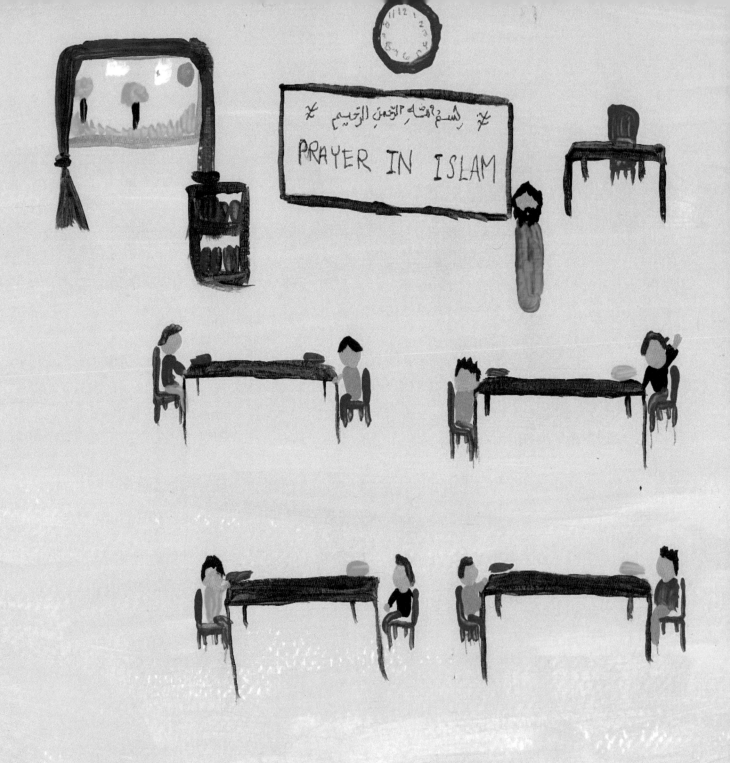

The next day, on Saturday morning, my mom knocked on my door.

'Time to wake up, son, it's time to get ready for your Weekend Islamic School,' said my mom.

When I got to class, my teacher announced, 'Today, we will be learning about Salah--- praying to Allah, the One that created us. Allah created us, so we can worship him. We worship him by praying our Salah prayers and doing things that please him like being good to our parents and helping others,' my teacher added.

'Who can tell me how many times Muslims pray in a day?' My teacher asked.

My friend, Omar, raised his hand and answered '6 times a day.'

'Not quite but close,' responded my teacher.

Then I remembered my dad going over this with me on our car ride back from the Mosque on Friday, so I raised my hand as high as I could.

'Yes, Zaid,' said my teacher as he pointed at me.

'Muslims pray five times a day,' I said.

'That is correct, Zaid, excellent!' replied my teacher with a smile on his face.

'Today's homework will be to find out when the five daily prayers are performed and write them down, and I'll need a brave someone to get up and present the times of the five daily prayers to the whole class,' said our teacher.

Riiiiiiiiing rang the bell as classes ended.

When I got home, I rushed to the kitchen to give my mom a hug, who was cooking lunch.

'How was school today, Zaid?' asked my Mom.

'It was interesting, Mom,' I replied. 'Our homework is to find out when Muslims pray the five daily prayers. Can you help me, Mom?'

'Of course, Zaid,' replied my mom as she was stirring the rice.

'The first is the **Fajr Prayer,** prayed from dawn to right before sunrise.

The second is the **Zuhr Prayer**, prayed just after noon (mid-day, when the sun passes the median point in the sky).

The third is the **Asr Prayer,** prayed during the afternoon (halfway between noon and sunset).

The fourth is the **Maghrib Prayer,** prayed directly after sunset.

The fifth is the **Isha Prayer**, prayed late evening, during the dark night (approximately an hour and a half after sunset).'

'Wow, Mom, that's a huge help,' I said. 'Now I'll need you to please repeat it, so I can write them down, memorize them, and hang them on my wall!' I added.

'Sure, Zaid,' replied my mom. 'But before you grab your notepad, I need to tell you one more thing,' Mom said as she seasoned our yummy chicken with salt and pepper.

'For a Muslim, when prayer time arrives, he or she is expected to stop what they are doing to pray to connect with Allah-- who is very near to us. We don't see Him, but He sees and hears us. Praying to Allah is for our own good and benefits us a lot in the afterlife and in this world too! A Muslim temporarily steps out of whatever activity he or she is doing, whether it's cooking, sleeping, or playing video games and prays to Allah. He needs to try his best to focus and concentrate during the Salah prayer and not let anything distract him or her-- every Muslim must work and practice to improve their prayer; it is a lifelong practice, do you understand me, Zaid?' asked Mom.'

'Yes, but it sounds a bit tough,' I replied.

'It may be a little tough in the beginning, but it gets easier, Zaid. Praying to God is a huge blessing and gift given to us from God!' said my Mom.

I smiled and ran to grab my notepad from my backpack.

My parents, sister, and I visit my uncle Nabeel, who is sick in the hospital.

'How are you feeling, Uncle Nabeel?' I asked my uncle.

'I am feeling a lot better, Zaid. Please keep me in your dua and ask Allah to restore my health,' my uncle replied.

'I will make dua for you when I am in prayer and outside of my prayers,' I said.

'Time for Uncle Nabeel to rest,' said the doctor as he walked in.

Then I kissed my uncle on his forehead, and we headed home.

The next day, my dad dropped me off at my best friend Omar's house. Omar has a soccer ball and a huge backyard where we usually play soccer. After we played, we went up to his room.

'What's this?' I asked my friend, Omar.

'It's a book my grandfather gave me,' Omar replied.

'What's it about, and what did you learn?' I asked Omar.

'It's about Salah—praying to Allah. The book taught me that Salah would be the first thing that Allah will ask us and judge us about on the Day of Judgment, Zaid. If one's prayer is in order, then everything else will fall into place,' added Omar.

'Wow, I did not know,' I replied.

'Now that it's time for the Asr prayer, let's pray together, Zaid,' said Omar. Maybe afterward, we can play some video games before dinner,' added Omar.

'Sounds like a plan,' I replied.

After we played some video games, it started to get dark, and I was getting a little hungry.

'Zaid, let's eat dinner, then pray Majrib with my dad,' said Omar.

We sat in the dining room table with Omar's parents in front of some delicious food and drinks. After we finished eating, it was time for us to pray together.

'Prayer is so sacred that one is not allowed to eat, drink, or talk when they pray. Did you know that, Zaid & Omar?' Omar's father asked us.

'Yes, we do,' we both replied. 'We learned that in class with our teacher,' we both said.

Then my dad came and took me home.

The next morning, my dad asked me, 'Zaid, do you want to take a run with me? I'll be jogging around the lake a few times,' added my dad

'Sure, Dad, let me put on my running shoes, and I'll meet you outside,' I replied.

My dad has been running for years, so he was a few steps ahead of me.

'Slow down, Dad,' I cried out.

My dad smiled as he slowed down for me.

'Zaid, look at all of Allah's beautiful creations-- SubhanAllah, look at all the beautiful big boggle-eyed frogs, pretty white ducks, and green hard-shelled turtles all around us. Allah is so amazing, He creating all these beautiful animals,' added my dad.

I stopped to catch my breath, I said Bismillah and took three sips of my water, then continued my jog with my dad.

Fast forward two years later. I noticed I went from praying once a day at the age of 7 to praying two to three times a day at the age of 8 and 9. I kept practicing and practicing. It was not easy, I had to sleep early at night, so I could get up early to pray Fajr in time. It was also not easy concentrating, especially for the Fajr prayer, since it was so early in the morning. But I kept reminding myself that I am doing this all for Allah so he can be pleased and happy with me and so that I could be a better person.

Salah acts as a spiritual diet. Like the body requires food and water throughout the day to be healthy, our spirit needs Salah, remembrance of Allah, and the worship of Allah to stay spiritually healthy. I also kept reminding myself that no matter how hard Salah gets, in the end, the journey is worth it because it's going to lead me to Paradise, where I will live forever and ever and wish for anything that I want.

Fast forward one more year, and here I am! 10 years old and Alhamdulillah, I can say I pray 5 times a day, every day! I even pray at Allah's House at our local Masjid here in my town every week and inshAllah soon, I'll be praying there every day! I feel great. Nothing beats connecting with Allah throughout the day. I noticed my prayers have transformed me into a better person. My attitude, behavior, mentality, thoughts, and priorities have all lined up to what really matters most in my life.

I try my best not to be lazy and skip my prayers because whenever someone gets lazy and skips their prayers, he or she will see the consequences of feeling distant from Allah--- which no one wants. It can cause someone to increase their sins and do bad things. Salah is my guard to all of that and my guard from Shaytan (devil) who whispers evil thoughts in people's ears!

'Zaid, wake up,' said my grandpa, waking me up in the middle of the night.

'Hi, Grandpa,' I responded as I try to open both my eyes.

'I am about to pray; do you want to join me? This is a special prayer called *'tahajjud'* that Allah loves very much,' Added my grandpa.

'Sure,' I responded as I got up and walked over to the washroom to make wudu.

Then I line up with my grandpa as he led us in prayer. We prayed for about 10 minutes; then I thanked my grandpa for waking me up and hopped back in bed.

I felt very close to Allah – as I prayed to him in the middle of the night. I was honored that Allah allowed me to pray in the middle of the night to Him, knowing it is not easy to do.

Allah has everything and does not need our worship or our prayers. We pray to benefit and help ourselves. God made worshipping Him and remembering Him beneficial to us--- so we should pray and remember Him all the time!

Thank you for taking this journey with me, and I hope you had just as much fun as I did down my memory lane. I hope you learned a thing or two and use this knowledge to connect with your Creator.

Remember, cherish your Salah because Salah is a huge gift that Allah has given you and me.

Salam Alaykum, friend!

Made in the USA
Coppell, TX
15 April 2021